1

What Was There All Along

Poems

Barbara McCauley Cardona

Alba Books Press

This edition copyright © 2015 Alba Books Press, USA

Text © 2015 Barbara McCauley Cardona
Cover Design © 2014 Barbara McCauley Cardona

ISBN-13: 978-0692553695
ISBN-10: 069255369X

Email: bcardona@cybermesa.com

Previous Publications

Finding the Balance, poems, Red Hill Press, San Francisco, CA, 1977. (Hughes)

12 Weeks to Better Vision, non-fiction, Pinnacle Books, New York, 1981. (Hughes)

Drug-Related Diseases, non-fiction, Franklin Watts, New York, 1987. (Hughes*)*

Small Mercies, memoir, Sherman Asher, Santa Fe, NM, 1998. (McCauley)

Destiny, historical romance, Alba Books Press, Truchas, NM, 2014. (McCauley Cardona)

Acknowledgments

Poems have appeared as follows:

The Nation, "Altadena Foothills."

Chelsea Review, "Old Woman."

Mendocino Review, " Fall Again."

Ann Arbor Review, "Folding the Wind In."

Visions, "Losing the Whales."

Northern Literary Review, "Between Seasons."

The Galley Sail Review, "Seizure," "Holding Together," "A Love Poem."

Milkweed Chronicle, "Light from the Whole Summer," "Trying on Your Death," "Entry," "Country Church," "The Season of Spring," "Fall Again," "The Bat," "Winter Light," "Write Me a Love Poem," "The Crossing."

The Beloit Poetry Journal, "The Party," "Pure Song."

Bachy 14, "Moving to Minnesota," "Dust From a Moth's Wing," "Learning to Pray."

Black Buzzard Review, "First Frost."

(Almost all of these poems appeared in the 80's and 90's under my former name of Barbara Hughes. Recent publications appear under my maiden name of Barbara McCauley, and, having discovered another writer of that name, all publications will now appear under Barbara McCauley Cardona.)

What Was There All Along

(Previously published as *The Darkness That Was There All Along*)

Poems by Barbara McCauley Cardona

(Cover photo of the poet's house in St. Paul, MN where most of these poems were written and which took the poet and her husband 10 years to renovate from a slumlord's rental to its original elegance.)

YEARS FROM NOW

Years from now, I will perhaps be
engrossed in something, like a book, a poem.
It will be late afternoon: the light enters
the room at an angle. I look up.
I am twenty years older
but there is that same sun
with the same golden dreams.
I see them so clearly:
those dreams
all lit up
in front of the shadows
I know now are what
brighten them.

MOVING TO MINNESOTA

Someone has lost a balloon.
Large and yellow, it lifts
first the trees
then, imperceptibly, the air itself, the snow.
I hang on
rise
with it, hovering above the branches.

This is how it is:
the sea is a thousand miles in one direction
two in the other.
I have lived on both sides.
Even now
it roars beneath the continent.

All day driving, the miles come in pieces.
It is hard to admire
the same hills for hours.
The weather surrounds me
comes in in drafts through the car windows
in through the dog's nose, she sniffs at it
behind my shoulder.
My feet are levers, my arms a steering wheel.
I am just leaving, just
arriving
my eyes this new landscape, still holding
what's left behind.

The house I liked

was just walls when
packed and sealed under gummed tape
our years of collecting, our fingernails, our spines
hauled it out, drained its life
stacked even the last week's dust
into the waiting truck
heading for
what we don't know about.

I'm higher than I want to be.
The string I hold worries me,
Below, the cities have disappeared.
The river twists like a ribbon
in an old woman's hair.

This house
groans with its history.
Footsteps are caught in the floorboards
echo back with each new footstep we make.
Grand old house, she's a
falling apart sloppy old woman
who wears unmatched socks rolled to the ankles
a baggy blouse with a button missing
where one tit hangs out dried like corn.
Already I love her.
She relinquishes her peeling paint
readies herself
with a sigh, says
welcome then.

To all of them:
Georgia with her belly growing a future.

Ameen with his hands that plant and harvest.
Holly who blossoms at night and with serious eyes
keeps track of the moon.
And Rosella her wise head that nods, *yes, yes*
I know what you mean. Go.
They follow me, hover in the luggage rack on top of the car
speak with the wind
Mel's voice the clearest through his bristling mustache
Georgia's a flute that whistles me on.

We form a small constellation
travelling north
stars, planets, Rachel, Helen, Jacqueline
my old French teacher
my mother, her smile askew, one eye wandering
my sister, my brother Tom.
Even the dead ones: my father, Lisa, Anthony.
We travel together, gather in the sky above Minneapolis.
Small lights alone
together we cast a pink glow at the edge of the river.

I descend.
The snow receives me.
I gather its diamonds
let them fall through my fingers
melt the coldness in the palm of my hand.
I dream my dream lovers under the arc of a streetlight
hold wet hands with the moon.
It is this way:
I enter my house.
I am finished with one thing
ready to start another.

WINTER SKIN

Snow this morning.
A set of footprints arrives at our door
as if one of us had come back in the night.
Everything is otherwise surface
its apparent perfection so much of our yearning
just as, in the sudden sun
we are lighted like candles,
like the cat in the window
a momentary fire.

The trees and bushes have gone anonymous
stripped down, except for the sparrows there
like old seed pods
puffed out, complaining.
Who's to blame them?
Nights they perch on the tops of the chimneys.
Some will make it, some not.
Do not pity them:
The newly dead travel fast.

LOSING THE WHALES

This morning, out the kitchen window
the leftover moon
is like a cataract
pale in the paler sky.
But somewhere now too, out on the sea
it floats like a lily
until a whale passes under
and the moon, for a moment
ripples into laughter.

The sun will come out today.
Like a fisherman it will cast our shadows
longer than ourselves, and blue against the snow.
Standing there
I will hear the chain saw from down the block
and the point of this day
of winter and what I am
will be felt in the deep drifts of my body.

But here in the kitchen now, I write in my journal.
How I am serene, calm
one with everything.
Behind me
suddenly, in the cabinets
the secret sound of chewing
the slightest disturbance
in the flatware.
It is a mouse.
My mind slams shut.
There is death in my saliva.

And so you see
this is how it happens:
all around me
the sky is emptying of the elms
where my vision used to land like a bird.
There is only the garage roof now
the house across the alley.
I watch one of them go down.
It spews twigs and branches
rises, drops
slapping hard
the face of the ocean.

THE BETRAYAL

Each morning it is different
this light that takes us by the hand
wraps us in its gauze like mummies
this, being light
alive.

Women stand in the shadows of your eyes.
They appear on street corners
snow caught in their eyelashes.
One pretends indifference
another she is a girl.
You take them all
distribute them the gift of your laughter.

Frost teases the branches into foliage.
White spring of delicate leaves and flowers.
The trees remain still
black.
They know the game
cannot be fooled.

Light is passed around
eaten at every table.
A communion of snowflakes
it falls on the tablecloth.
With all of its promises
melts.

How simple is this light.
How it holds us without feeling.
As when you hold me now
I feel the fire from far away.
This light is in me.
We pass through it as through a room.
Make of it our lives.

A LOVE POEM

The night you leave
leaves
snow.
Winter sets in just like that.
And your being gone
is suddenly
the way I am out here
with the dog
and the carpenter who is wrapped in layers up on the eaves.
He hammers
his breath solid as the cloud overhead
stops his work to show me
a dusky bird.
Cardinal, he says, *female.*
I see her, a leaf high on the dead elm.
He is closing the soffits today.
The yellow insulation sticks out along the edge
like a new nest just under the roof.

It is not that I want you here just now.
It is that I discover
the dimensions of our rooms.
The coleus, the empty piano
how I caress
the sound of the snow plow
the whole night's dogs.

Today our dog runs with the others
who are out as she is
celebrating

churning up snow in tight circles.
Today on the blue shadow of a branch on the snow
a female cardinal hangs on.
The neighbor's cupola cuts sharply into the sky.
The night you leave leaves me
and you
wherever you are
this incredible sunlight
touching both our shoulders.

OBJECTS IN THE MORNING

The flower pot is white, charred at the base
bellies out, then in to the thin neck
caressing the baby's breath
that rises from its mouth like smoke.

The fan rests on the table
wings still
the slightest trembling in its machine heart
while on the floor last night's pillow
seeks to unlump itself.
The rocker
unmoving
presides like a judge.

Clearly these things know themselves:
the pot with its fissure
into which, someday
it will disappear
this door that just creaks
when I lean on it.

THE BAT

In the winter darkness, they are under the eaves
their small furry bodies
wrapped tight
in the leather of their wings.

The sun pours through the squares of the bathroom window
lies flat on the wood floor, pretending a warmth
that belongs instead to the radiator.
The house is silent around me.
I prepare for a bath
prepared
as I like to think
for anything.

In summer you can see them
like swallows or huge moths
flitting against the last evening light.
Dark angels, they carry the night on their shoulders.
Really, they are bats.
Rodents with wings, without tails.
Who knows what they are?
Sooner or later
fear finds a home in the eyes
widens in the dark pupils, freezes there
into schedules, my morning bath
a cup of tea, the mailman, a train that arrives on time.
Fear is the name of what is not named
the shadow that rises behind every word.
Like the bat
it is blind.

The water from the faucet
splashes against the sink
lets go of my hands.
Its icy welcome travels up the pipes
emptying itself, holding nothing.
It becomes whatever color is around it.
Water is not fear.

I pull open the shower curtain.
Something moves in the corner of my eye.
I want to name it. It is an animal
a frog, a mouse, I can't believe it.
It is winter, they are hibernating.
It is small, would fit in the palm of my hand.
Its head moves slightly from side to side.
It is because its wings are in
that I cannot name it.
I feel the menace of its silence.
I can't kill it. I can't love it.

This morning sun does not fool me.
Behind my disbelief, all reasoning
behind the now-closed door
it is there:
        this bat that has lived inside me
curled a long time in its sleep.
It has always been there
but I do not know this yet.
It is only after
I have asked a friend
to catch it, to bottle it

the mayonnaise jar I give him
that will slowly smother it.
The days I will avoid its presence
pretending I do not feel
its slow dying inside me.
It is only after all this
when I look finally at its stillness
what I see
is a bat
dead inside a jar.
And I know now it was useless.
Its brothers are curled up beneath the roof.
They breathe slowly, deeply
waiting for the thaw.

ENTRY

Tonight I feel close to my death.
Curious, like an outsider
I hang around
keeping my distance, but
letting it settle alongside.

A yellow alley cat
uses our backyard sometimes as home.
Has seduced the dog into accepting him.
Last summer the cat
leaped into my lap
as I lounged in the sun.

It is that way with death.
That strange fur I wasn't sure of.
Flattered that he would trust me
worried he might strike out
that I might startle him into it
inadvertently.

Tonight I feel close to my death.
I don't seek it, but tonight
it is here, totally absorbing
pulling me in its tide
the white moon reflected back
from the snow.

HOLDING TOGETHER

The *I Ching* says the correct place of the woman
is within
that of the man without.
And it means what it says.
Just as in two months more
the snow will shrink back along the sidewalks
and everything then but water
will hold its breath
the sky itself furrowed with clouds as though
vaguely remembering
these swelling buds
the grackle's loud doorbell.

The order of it, that is the surprise.
The uncovering of the laws:
that a black hole can only expand, that is its nature.
That it swallows itself down to an unimaginable smallness.
The paradox.
Like us, how we hold together
our laughter hoisted out like the neighbor's laundry
steamy in the crisp winter air.

THE CROSSING

The winter was a wide prairie
an immense whiteness that took the color from our eyes.
The first signs now are in the distance.
The clouds have gathered there like messengers crowding in.
We feel the softening in the air and ground
can, for the first time
look behind us.
It is over.
And we look again
at each other
with something like sunlight in our eyes.

It wasn't always like this.
We lived many years
in the spring of another country
trusted the green that surrounded us, laughed together
yet all the while
the roots choked in the clay
the desert it was it would one day return to
though you were the only one ever knew it.

Oh, in your eyes this winter I have said goodbye
and seen it
a tall thin soldier standing guard.
And there too, as now
with the branches still bare against the sky
I see the promise, hear it.
How something has happened
an imperceptible breaking
a parting in the prairie grass

of the new shoots.

You, and the green waxy leaves of the tropics
and I with my cool northern eyes.
Together we have come to this slight thaw
aware now of the seasons between us.
And you and the rain
this rising warmth that melts the snow
the two of us
with moons in the same sky
our hearts, our voices
one slow
one fast
how we have become this old snow
right now
that is melting
that is becoming
simple
water.

BETWEEN SEASONS

Our hats hang on the halltree
abandoned above the coats and scarves
like a band of hoboes
around the small fire of sunlight
that comes in through the narrow windows.

Gutters, with only memories of snow
chatter endlessly up and down the street
while here, in the entry hall
where I pause
dust motes
flicker in the silence.
I needn't listen.
They have nothing to say.

THE SEASON OF SPRING

Grandma will be 86 this year
and every once in a while she mentions
that door at the end of her life
which we close quickly with a word or a look.
She is not half so afraid as we are and listens
when a friend tells how he thinks a foetus must die
in order to be born into this life.
He makes it sound easy
and we are grateful
though apparently only for Grandma.

What do you think of that? she asks.
Do you think it's true
that we die to be born again something new?
She's Catholic as I was once
and *born again* sounds awfully Protestant.
It sounds wonderful, I say, *I like it.*
And I do, it's true, you see
we lived like dolphins once in the small oceans of our
                                                    mothers.

The cottonwood across the street rolls in the wind.
Like a huge dog it shudders
shaking out its loose fur.
Grandma and I watch
as the seeds sail out
riding the air
to land wherever the wind drops them.

OLD WOMAN

She comes to this park every day.
Here she tells me
my hands are bread.

FROM THE FIFTH FLOOR OF THE ST. PAUL HOTEL

I will try to catch for you
what it was up there that day
seen from the window
that makes me want to find it again.
The roofs below looked like fields
flat
square
puddles lay in them like cows.

I'd like to show you
how it is
to exactly shape whatever it was up there that day:
straight down a small window on the wood roof shed
catches the wind and
opens
hangs a moment, then half-closes
closes.
It keeps on doing that
and I imagine how the air will travel downstairs
and in a few minutes the dust on the landing two floors down
will stir
just a little.

It was a day the river and sky
spilled out of each other.
In the distance the somber hills and mansions of St. Paul
presided above trees
that rollicked in the gusts of wind
bursting into sudden laughter.

I stood there watching for no reason
except I liked the way the one red roof looked against the sky.
You know how it is: these particular moments when we seem
to reach for something
a small music or words that are shadows of what cast them
just as when the whales sing
only parts of their sounds reach us.
The rest soar through an immense silence
inside the pocket of another silence.

DEATH OF A DOG

Outside in the garden on this first warm day
I decide the sun might help the dog
and so I go to get her, carry her downstairs
out of the room where she's lain for three days
just lying there, her breathing the only anchor left
and put her beside me on the grass.

She is thin, dried out
like these weeds I've pulled that, nevertheless
held on
breaking free only with effort
with a sound of tearing.
Again, I think how I hadn't planned on this
how maybe she'll make it

She tries to rise, move away.
I miss the point and move next to her
then watch
as the thin resilient roots
break along her spine
moving up to the quivering nose
where something
hesitates
as if momentarily
confused
then definitely
sails out
letting her body sink
like soil
into the space
left behind.

LEARNING TO PRAY

Finding it again
with a difference
the voice that lifts in praise
the voice that asks for
not for itself and not to
deities
but for the thing itself.

Finding it in the small things because
I have studied the landscape of maps
names that don't name.
It is difficult to begin.
The voices of everything are whispers
I can barely hear.

Two years ago there was a girl
named Liz.
She was one of us
she was a poet, a butterfly.
One night the fine powder that gave her flight
dropped on the carpet, became dust.
A hush surrounded her.
It was the sound of everything else
breathing.

She lay in the hospital for days.
Machines defined her
showed only flat lines, no curves
as if her brain had melted inside her

leaving a puddle of just one thought.
It was then I understood praying:
we would circle her, our hands together
our voices one we would ask her to return.
I didn't mention this.
They turned the machines off.

Each day I break the spines of lettuce
feel them crack between my fingers.
I peel onions and garlic
cut through their pungent flesh.
I was never taught to thank them.
In my awkward way
when I am sure no one is around
I whisper to their beautiful bodies.

This praying is like that fat robin
who sits on a branch outside my kitchen window.
He catches the sun on his sun's breast
gives it back with a song that comes easy.
I try it:
a thin whistle that is not mine
not even like his.
It is this reaching out that will find it
the part of me that can do it.
Any moment now.

ALTADENA FOOTHILLS

Frogs
with their rainbows of sound,

What I can't see in the ravine below
I know must be moist.

FOLDING THE WIND IN

A song of grass
for no reason, the crickets
do a better job, the spider whose web
melts in the morning sun. An ant
knows grass better than I
in its way
with tiny
arms.

Singing to bring
the wash in with
wet
blades stuck in the arch
of my foot. The singing
there
in the shadow of my body's weight
sprung back in an instant: a song.
And in the singing
that
that a big white cloud
sails over.

REFLECTION IS OUR OTHER BODY

The sun hangs above the horizon facing me
repeats itself clearly in the water below.
Two suns looking at me.
If it weren't for the opposite shore
lake and sky would merge.

A mist hangs over the water on the other side.
The one heron on this shore
is its gathering into a solid cloud.
He watches us as we approach
prepares to leave
and does
flying low across the water.
His wings break the smooth surface
as though his shadow did it.

I run
my friend beside me.
Ducks in the shallows stand on their heads
tails straight up like strange flowers growing.
A coot
drops anchor beneath the surface.

Each day it is different.
The blossoms have come to fullness
one morning, from only the slightest pink aura
to a glow that burst out as does now the sun dropping
confetti on the path.

Lilacs, birds, another runner.
it is this way:
this morning we don't talk.
We run
feel our muscles, one foot after the other.

The cottonwood
shows how easy it is
as does the air
that opens and closes
and the water that gives for the mallard
when he slides down into it.

And so this morning we keep running
around and around the lake.
The day grows. The sun rises, falls
to become a moon.
Darkness edges the lake, the swans
rise up as we pass, our footsteps drumbeats, by midnight
the only sound other than one car
on its way home.

We run
two women
husbands, children, rooms abandoned.
We sleep running.
We know the way perfectly, each
curve, each break in the path.
The trees pass us onward round and round
until morning again, the sun
just as it was yesterday
only it isn't, it is

how we are
when the man on the opposite shore sees us:
two women
in the water
running across the sun.

PURE SONG

For Dorothy Purves

At last.
You have died.
No more of that body caught like a weed
against a windy fence.
No more the inarticulable words
the burned-out bridge between mind and tongue.
I don't even cry.
I applaud you.
just when we thought you'd never do anything
you did it.
You left.
And I imagine you now, hiding your laughter behind one hand
as your new body moves
each airy limb.
You try it out
tentative, as when a girl
the first time on a two-wheeler
you wobbled down the road.
But you learned the trick
as now
look at you
big show-off.

DUST FROM A MOTH'S WING

The green melon
even in darkness green.
How light must filter through its walls
like sun into a chapel.
It knows itself.
I cut it. It gives.

Six of them come in through the back door
big men, their faces red with pleasure.
The children are in the attic
with orders to be silent.
Their eyes big.

The gun is difficult.
I've never used it.
I pull the hammer back.
The door is broken through.
There is no sound
as I pull the trigger.
The first one falls grasping his chest.
One by one they round the corner
one by one they fall
lie there
then get up. It begins again.
The children are in the attic.
They don't move as I have told them.

I am preparing meat:
a leg of lamb that spits in the oven

fills the kitchen with smoke.
I have stuffed pieces of garlic into the flesh
this dead meat we eat with rice and prunes
with a friend, a woman whose smile
is like a bird always
ready for flight.

The authorities arrive at the home of Neruda
his corpse on the bed.
They search his house by the sea, break its walls
expecting more of him
something he may have left in the seams of his books
or in the dust that has gathered on the window ledges.
They break the bindings
listen to the air around him.
Unexpected
a few words escape his lips.
This is what they've come for.

I call for the cat.
For three days now we haven't seen him.
The fourth day I stop calling.
The cat appears in my dream.
I reach up to him
but he disappears.

Tonight it is bullets again.
I crouch in the chair by the window
try to read my book.
I wish to appear nonchalant.
It is just these things that pull them toward me
this mind I lean on.

I sink into it finally
move to another chair
out of range.

She wants to touch you.
Her hair is carefully combed
clothes just right.
She vanishes somewhere in her new soft voice
or is it the language she's invented to hide in?

I don't mean to be secret about this, it's just
that everyone has given up on the cat.
He's dead.
A part of me has been cut away.
How is it then on the ninth day
we hear him?
He looks up at me from behind the garage wall.
He has come home.
His hind legs drag.
He has pulled himself home.

The body is sometimes its own coffin
and the way out, it seems
could be anywhere.
Your voice lifts upward, beyond what is at first
believed to be
then recognized
as your own pulse.

THE TREE

Out in the lawn chairs in the sun, warm at last
our voices float out into the wind like the seeds of the
                                       cottonwood
into the neighbors' yards.
We are facing the maple you transplanted two years ago
tied down at an angle, in hopes it will miss
the electrical line you forgot about
when you moved it.
You tell me about a woman at the party who
looking at your paintings
told you she didn't like abstractions.
We sit quietly.
The maple's arms are askew, reaching everywhere
as if it hasn't quite figured out where it is going.

Tree, I say like a child with her primer.
Tree, and it becomes one
interchangeable with the birch further away.
I erase the word, just look.
A green madness is about to topple at my feet.
Across the street the cottonwood quivers with applause.
It is the last tall angel above our houses
the elms ghosts now
remembered mainly by the mushrooms that sprout in circles
where they used to stand.

Tree, and the child's wonder gets neatly folded
like underwear into the waiting drawer.
Tree, the word a net to catch this fish
language the web in which the spider of consciousness dangles.

This tree struggles to find its way upward
its roots travelling through an opaque sea.

This tree will outlive me.
Your painting is the same mystery, I say, the same fish.
But this is the real world:
leaf, limb, branch, twig, bud, flower.
You laugh at my arguments.
A gust of wind carries your laughter up
over the neighborhood.

AFTER SURGERY

Today, the moment's a wide blue
and I'm taking it in like a bee at the hollyhocks.
A gulp of beer, a swig of raspberry bushes
their fruit glowing like some living proof.
They're so smug
raspberry bushes.
Irritation rises with everything else's perfection.
Oh today, what is it?
My belly is healing the scar of a slag heap
cut into, mined, my body so seemingly separate.
I want it to wander, it won't
insists on remaining, so here I am
hot, sticky, in a plastic lawn chair
while something in me flits mad with the cabbage moth
sways in the maple.
Me here
like that cloud with its fat bottom
suddenly blocking the sun

SUMMER NIGHT

The dogs come in, sniffing at the corners of the room
settle between us, where we sit in the dusk
in the crooked rythmn of the rocking chair.
We don't turn on the lights, no.
Tonight we let everything fade
even ourselves
as if tonight
the past can be rolled up like a carpet
to be put away.
The last thing to go
is the blue plate by the window.
It lingers as long as the song of a neighbor child
reaching us from behind the hedge across the street
tuneless, intimate
like so many of the things we have done
in order to survive.

HIDE AND SEEK

I am 'it' in the 9 o'clock dusk
my head against the apple tree
counting like a hypnotist.

You know how it is:
At first you hear all your friends running away
then, no matter how fast you count
silence stretches out taut in every direction
so when at last you turn
you dangle
lone spider
in the fog-falling night.

A firefly flashes on and off.
In the warm breeze
the peonies bob
whitely
in the dark.

LOOKING FOR SOMETHING TO SAY

It was out there with you and the children
visiting the grave, each of us
aware of our feet there, and her name
and the month and the year.
I wanted to say something
for the children perhaps
something about
the one bird I heard
pumping its song out over the hillside
or the sunlight, the valley that leaned against the foothills
with orange trees full of their fruit that even from this far
was glowing.
It was
the contrast, her being
there
and the song suddenly cut off
by the sound of three men with their shovels.

You put flowers from our garden in the vase that was there for
                                                    them.
We left then, talked about the unusual weather
the way it was, how what I couldn't find
was left
with a bird, a stone, the sound of those shovels
her smile, her gestures.

DAUGHTER, GROWN-UP

The clouds yawn and the sun comes out.
Cows, if they could, would fly upside down
to investigate the undersides of clover.
In the middle of this
as usual
you call
I won't be home tonight.

The quiet of the house settles
like the night
into every corner.
The cat
curls
into the pockets of your unmade bed.

LIGHT FROM THE WHOLE SUMMER

Something in my face has changed
the way the trees each autumn
burst out
visible and final
before they withdraw into themselves
around the curled, sleeping animals.

My hair flames white at the edges
as if the light inside
has filled me up and I glow
light spilling out
even to my fingertips.

This aging is a story
we only half believe
Who says it's terrible?
It's a gathering
a wave come to fullness
that rushes back again to the sea.

When I look back at the shore
the footsteps are already gone.
The sea breathes
Failure is no longer endless
in front of me.

FALL AGAIN

The sky is losing itself in the horizon.
The shadows are eating the grass.
Each day now is a glass of thirsty water
drinking.
You listen to how out of the tangle of roots, of dying
how out of yourself, the season comes
dull like the wings of a crow just lifting
heavy like that.

A Jerusalem cricket came in last night
shellacked and shiny like a new shoe in the corner.
Killed, I could see the mess he would make
so I caught him in a jar and put him outside
then dreamed I was struck by lightning
a thread of light that had no end in the sky above me.
It was meant for someone else, but I begged for it
believing it to be a blessing.
It knocked me down
nearly killed me.

The heat has dried itself out.
It has shrunk into the leaves of the cottonwood tree
falls like the feathers of a dead bird all around you.
You sit in the garden. Your voice, like the silence
settles into the ground.
The days move out
packing the light up with them.

WRITE ME A LOVE POEM

It doesn't count
when you have to ask for it
is what I say
about love poems.
But every time you go away
I think
maybe this time.
And now you're gone again.
You have little to do
the hours empty barrels you poke around in.
Write to me.
Put on paper all the things you've said to me.
I want it in writing.
Think of it this way:
the wind just blows
across that prairie.

THE VIOLENCE OF THE DOGS

The dogs sleep with the sun curled into warm fur
until I call them, and want stretches their bodies.
Deliciously they are leap
grass
the one stick they both must have.
Are teeth
that suddenly mean it.

And it's over.
The little one bellies up
and the other shakes herself
with one last look, walks away.
They will lie separately for a while.
Like us after an argument.
That space we keep crossing.

I have seen them do this before
and today is not different
not for them.
It is for me to see in their violence
how little I have dared to love
how much I dread the little I do.
Like this 5 o'clock light with its going shadows.

TRYING ON YOUR DEATH

Your shirt taken off inside out
lies in a heap on the floor.
The sun angling in through the window
folds itself into its pockets.
You breathe beside me, we've made love
each of us still
a pulse of the other.

You say how you are tired
not in the usual way
and that you've dreamed of dying.
You say this with reluctance.
I watch the patterns of dust
rising and falling in the light.

You're trying on your death, I say.
I have too, just as I've tried on yours
and you, mine
to see how it feels.
You don't laugh
or look away
and I recall my childhood home
with its hedge the boundary of our yard
demarcating woods from garden.

This long soft afternoon, snowflakes begin to fall
lazy like ourselves.
I taste the edge of the crysanthemums I cut today
a bitterness

sudden
on the back of my tongue.

FIRST FROST

In the air of early autumn
even here in the middle of the continent
there is something of the ocean
felt in the slow tilt
as the earth lowers into the north
seaweed dragging after it
the shore stripped and harvested.

Riding the back of the wind
the first geese are leaving.
They are so high up
their cries trail behind them.
Somewhere down here
their tiny shadows skim the land
crossing the roads and gullies
flickering on the ripening apples.

THE PARTY

Whole pears, skinned like fish, float in their liquid.
Chinese porcelain and silver, the polished table in candlelight.
My friend serves at one end, her face soft and smiling
the room itself a painting we have entered
with our noisy lives, our impertinence.

She gives us this, one clear cold night
a warmth with a shape we can settle into.
In her hands, the hours become bread.
They rise, give off delicious odors.
We can hardly believe that our hungers wait
like our boots, at the door.

When it's over, I embrace her.
Her body trembles against mine, and not with laughter.
So strange, I think, after such ease, such perfection.
so familiar, I wonder if it's not myself.
And am grateful, relieved, for this final touch
like the fire burning down now, and the stars so far away
also trembling
giving themselves that way.

THE DAY YOU SHOT YOUR DOG

In the middle of the lake with its old bass, his one blind eye.
A trembling at the edge of the lake, it was
a kindness.
The only sound
in the forest.

SEIZURE

It begins in the belly
as if there were a drain there
from which the plug has been pulled.
And down I go, water from a tub
the floor the last solid edge
before I am sucked out.

I remember the floors:
one in a liquor store in Mexico
its tiles some geometric mystery
directing me to a piece of chewing gum
flattened into a dirty moon;
another floor that came smack up against a wall
with dust rollers, slow-moving clouds;
and you somewhere above calling me
to come back, come back.

It is not unpleasant for me.
I remember nothing once I go.
It is later
the way your eyes don't quite
meet mine, don't quite
tell me, when I ask, how bad it was
guarded with gentleness and erasure
the way after smaller disasters
how we all assure ourselves
it wasn't so terrible after all
here we are, intact.

I like to list others: the famous ones
line them up like ancestors.
Dostoevsky and I, for example
I like the sound of that.
And sometimes I think I am an angel perhaps
with pressing business elsewhere
so that I leave, must leave
anytime, in the middle of anywhere
my body a puppet, suddenly idiotic
on the untended strings.

THE HARVEST

The sunlight filters through the curtain
and, with its lace, lies flat up against the wall, like paint.
Outside in the garden
the blue of the sky falls
into the collar of your workshirt
down to the deeper tone of your jeans.

The shadows of everything deepen
yawn across the grass, gathering the darkness
that was there all along.
Our house crosses the street, climbs up the neighbor's.
When it reaches the top
the corner steeple will be the last candle.
You break off an eggplant
straighten.
A small sun is setting in your eyes
when you turn toward me, and look.

COUNTRY CHURCH

Those who are buried
are not done with this life.
and so I will be buried
face west
where my life has gone
each day, with the sun
the clock of my blood.

This place could be anywhere
happens
to be here
now, with trees that drop colors
as if they were real.
I will never come here again.
It is one of those places
a landscape that carries me
from one place to another
exists only today
with the wind.

We have our picnic
under the yellow elm
whose leaves and branches
bend to the coming winter.
Our eyes take in what is here:
the abandoned church
empty of what lies now to the west of it:
small congregation of stones
of gingham skirts
scouring and sweeping.

Even now
the churchyard is clean
swept by this wind that just pushes
its fingers through our hair
fills us
with the light only today has given.

Death, what is it?
A quickness.
What is left
to be taken in a new way.
Today
just today
I feel the broken body of my dream.
It billows up in the wind
saluting whatever is to come.

www.ingramcontent.com/pod-product-compliance
Lightning Source LLC
Chambersburg PA
CBHW060428090426
42734CB00011B/2486